Tough Topics

Drugs

Ana Deboo

Heinemann Library
Chicago, Illinois

Photo research by Erica Martin and Ginny Stroud-Lewis
Designed by Richard Parker and Q2A Creative
Printed and bound in China by South China Printing Company

11 10 09 08 07
10 9 8 7 6 5 4 3 2 1

Library of Congress Cataloging-in-Publication Data
Deboo, Ana.
  Drugs / Ana Deboo.
    p. cm. -- (Tough topics)
  Includes bibliographical references and index.
  ISBN 978-1-4034-9736-9 -- ISBN 978-1-4034-9741-3 (pbk.)
  1. Drug abuse--Juvenile literature. I. Title.
  HV5809.5.D43 2007
  613.8--dc22
                        2007002789

Acknowledgments
The author and publisher are grateful to the following for permission to reproduce copyright material:
Alamy Images pp. **6** (oote boe), **10** (Bob Pardue), **12** (Darrin Jenkins), **15** (Photofusion Picture Library), **17** (ImageState/Pictor International), **19** (john rensten), **24** (ACE STOCK LIMITED); Art Directors and Trip pp. **13**, **14**, **18**; Corbis pp. **20**, **21**, **27** (Zefa/Roy Morsch); Getty Images pp. **4** (Stone/Phil Degginger), **16** (Stone/Bruce Gardner), **22** (Photodisc), **23** (Stone/Penny Tweedie), **25** (Taxi/Michael Tamborrino), **26** (Photonica/Seth Goldfarb), **28** (Photographer's Choice/Kaz Mor), **29** (Stone/David Harry Stewart); Science Photo Library pp. **5**, **7** (Robert Isear), **8** (Scott Camazine), **9**.

Cover photograph reproduced with permission of Getty Images/ The Image Bank/ Malcolm Piers.

Every effort has been made to contact copyright holders of any material reproduced in this book. Any omissions will be rectified in subsequent printings if notice is given to the publisher.

Contents

Drug Dangers

Drugs are around us all the time. Some drugs help us, like **medicines**. We take medicines when we are sick or to stay healthy.

▼Pharmacies are stores that have medicines.

►Illegal drugs can be in the form of powders, pills, or dried plants.

Some drugs are against the law because they can be dangerous. They can cause heart attacks, breathing problems, or other health issues. Legal drugs can be dangerous if they are used in the wrong way.

What Are Drugs?

▲ All tobacco products contain a drug called nicotine.

A drug is any **chemical** that is used to change the way the brain and body work. Drugs can be swallowed or **inhaled** through the mouth or nose. Some drugs are injected with a needle or rubbed onto the skin.

Many drugs are made from plants. Other drugs, like aspirin, are created by mixing man-made chemicals. Some drugs have mild **effects**, such as the calamine lotion you rub on a rash to make it stop itching. Stronger drugs can have powerful effects on the mind and body.

◄ Legal drugs are made at factories.

Drugs in History

Drugs have been around for a very long time. People probably discovered their **effects** while testing which plants were safe to eat. Several different drugs are made from a flower called the opium poppy.

▶ The opium poppy was used as medicine by the ancient Greeks.

▶Fibers from some kinds of hemp plants can be used to make ropes or fabric.

Nearly 5,000 years ago, people in China were using the leaves of a hemp plant as **medicine**. The illegal drug **marijuana** is still made from that plant.

Medicines

If a drug improves or cures a physical or mental problem, it is called a **medicine**. Some medicines are sold over-the-counter. This means that people can buy them at any time and choose for themselves when to use them.

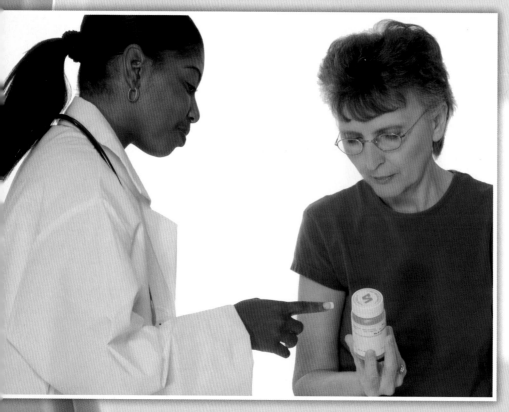

◀ Follow the doctor's instructions when taking prescription drugs.

> ▶Read the label before taking any medicine.

Drug Facts

Warnings

Alcohol warning: If you consume 3 or more alcoholic drinks every day, ask your doctor whether you should take acetaminophen or other pain relievers or fever reducers. Acetaminophen may cause liver damage.

Sore throat warning: If sore throat is severe, persists for more than 2 days, is accompanied or followed by fever, headache, rash, nausea, or vomiting, consult a doctor promptly.

Do not use
- with any other product containing acetaminophen
- if you are now taking a prescription monoamine oxidase inhibitor (MAOI) (certain drugs for depression, psychiatric or emotional conditions, or Parkinson's disease), or for 2 weeks after stopping the MAOI drug. If you do not know if your prescription drug contains an MAOI, ask a doctor or pharmacist before taking this product.

Ask a doctor before use if you have
- heart disease
- high blood pressure
- thyroid disease
- diabetes
- trouble urinating due to an enlarged prostate gland
- persistent or chronic cough such as occurs with smoking, asthma or emphysema
- cough that occurs with too much phlegm (mucus)

When using this product do not exceed recommended dosage

Stop use and ask a doctor if
- nervousness, dizziness, or sleeplessness occurs
- pain, nasal congestion or cough gets worse or lasts for more than 7 days

Drug Facts (continued)
- fever gets worse or lasts for more than 3 days
- redness or swelling is present
- new symptoms occur
- cough comes back or occurs with rash or headache that lasts

These could be signs of a serious condition.

If pregnant or breast-feeding, ask a health professional before use.

Keep out of reach of children.

Overdose warning: Taking more than the recommended dose (overdose) may cause liver damage. In case of overdose, get medical help or contact a Poison Control Center right away. Quick medical attention is critical for adults as well as for children even if you do not notice any signs or symptoms.

Directions

Do not take more than directed (see overdose warning)

Adults and children 12 years and over
- take 2 caplets every four hours
- do not take more than 12 caplets in 24 hours
- swallow whole - do not crush, chew or dissolve

Children under 12 years
- do not use this adult product in children under 12 years of age; this will provide more than the recommended dose (overdose) and may cause liver damage.

Other information
- store between 20 - 25° C (68 - 77° F)
- do not use if carton is opened or if blister unit is broken
- see side panel for expiration date.

Some medicines are sold only when a doctor decides a person needs them. These are called **prescription** medications.

Common Drugs

◄People may take the drug marijuana by smoking the dried leaves of the plant.

Tobacco and alcohol are common drugs that are legal for adults to use. The most common illegal drug is **marijuana**, also called pot or cannabis. Other illegal drugs include **ecstasy**, **cocaine**, **heroin**, and **LSD**.

One kind of illegal drug that some people **abuse** is called **anabolic steroids**. Some athletes take steroids because they can help their muscles get stronger and bigger. Steroids can also make a person moody or violent.

▶It is against the rules to use steroids in any sport.

Drug Abuse

▶Marijuana can make people feel tired.

Most drug **abuse** happens when people use drugs to change the way they feel. People may hope to feel calmer, happier, or more energetic. But they often feel worse when the drug has worn off.

▲Alcohol is a legal drug that is sometimes abused.

Some people take drugs to escape their problems. While they are on the drug, they may forget what is upsetting them. But drugs do not make problems go away. They can make them worse over time.

Drug Addiction

Many drugs are **addictive**. The person using a drug begins to want and need the drug. Scientists think an addict's brain changes so that the body feels as if it will not work without the drug.

◄Some **prescription** drugs are addictive.

▶ Many addicts want to stop using drugs but feel sick when they do not take them.

When a person becomes addicted to something, the body gets used to it. Addicts have to take more of a drug to feel the **effects** or just to feel normal.

Harmful Effects of Drugs

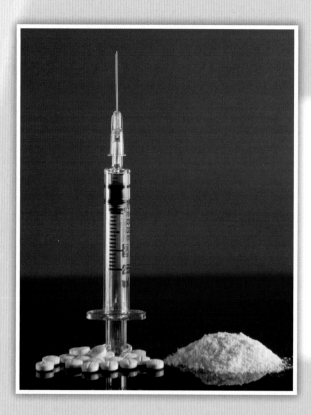

◄When people inject drugs with used needles, they can become infected with diseases.

Some health problems are caused by the way a drug is taken. Drugs that people smoke leave solid particles (pieces) in the lungs that can eventually cause cancer and other health problems.

Drugs can change the way the brain and body work. This makes it more likely that users will have accidents. Drugs can also have harmful **side effects**. For example, **cocaine** speeds up the heart and can cause heart attacks.

▼Cocaine is usually **inhaled** as a powder.

Overdoses

One of the most serious dangers with drugs is taking an **overdose**. This means that there is too much of the drug in the body.

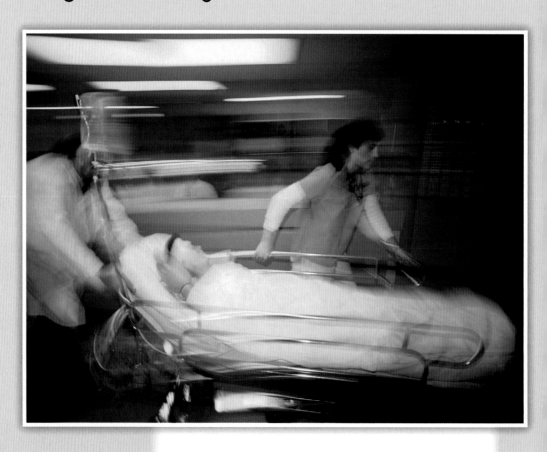

▲An overdose can cause a **coma** or death.

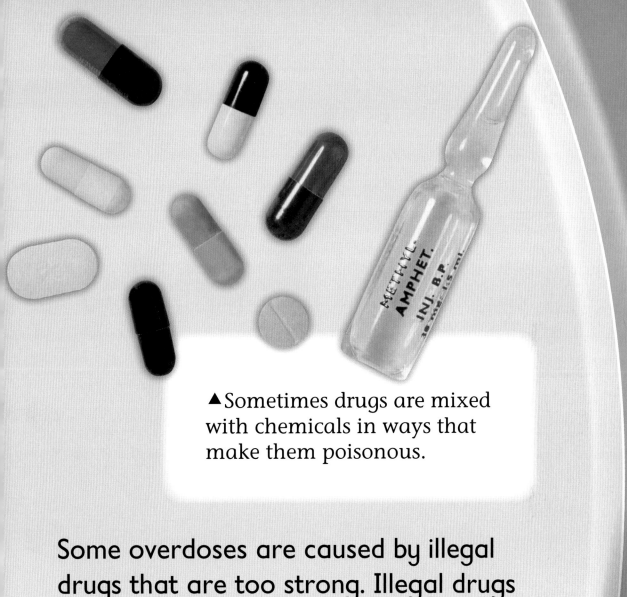

▲Sometimes drugs are mixed with chemicals in ways that make them poisonous.

Some overdoses are caused by illegal drugs that are too strong. Illegal drugs are often made by people who do not know about **chemicals**. They might use cheap ingredients so they have more of the drug to sell.

Emotional Effects

◄ Drug addicts may have trouble paying for food and housing.

Drug **abuse** can harm people's lives in many ways. Drugs can be expensive. Many drug users cannot afford to buy drugs and take care of their everyday needs.

People who are addicted to drugs may have trouble focusing. They may end up losing their job or dropping out of school.

◄ Drugs can make people feel all alone.

Drugs and the Law

It is against the law to make, sell, or use illegal drugs. A person can be arrested just for having them.

◀ It is against the law to use another person's **prescription** medication.

►People can go to jail for having small amounts of drugs.

The punishment for breaking these laws can be very strict. People caught breaking a drug law can serve time in prison even if it was their first crime.

Kids and Drugs

▶Some young people may try drugs to fit in with their friends.

Many young people want to try new things. Some think drugs will help them escape their problems. But drugs can cause harm that lasts much longer than the fun.

It is always smart to learn more before you decide whether or not to try something. Find out as much as you can about drugs before you take the risk.

▲Friends should support your choice not to take drugs.

Where to Go for Help

If you know someone who **abuses** drugs, there are ways to get help. There are telephone hotlines to call, where counselors can offer advice. You can find more information on the Internet or in a phone book under "drug abuse information."

▶ Talk to a trusted adult about the best ways to help friends who abuse drugs.

▶Support groups can help family members deal with their loved one's drug addiction.

Many drug users are able to quit once they realize drugs are harming their lives. There are medical clinics and support groups for people who are addicted to drugs. Friends and family can help, but people must decide for themselves that they need to quit.

Glossary

abuse use carelessly or in the wrong way

addictive able to make people feel a strong need for something

anabolic steroid drug that can make muscles bigger and stronger, and can also cause mood problems

chemical matter that can be created by or is used in scientific processes

cocaine drug made from the coca plant that is inhaled

coma unconsciousness caused by injury, disease, or drug use

ecstasy drug that affects the workings of the brain over time. Ecstasy is taken as a pill.

effect change brought on by something

heroin drug made from opium poppies that is injected with a needle

inhale breathe in through the nose or lungs

LSD drug made from a chemical that can change how people see things. It can create frightening feelings and other unwanted side effects.

marijuana drug made from a plant that is smoked

medicine drug used to improve, prevent, or cure a physical or mental problem

overdose large amount of a drug that can cause illness or death

prescription written order from a doctor that allows the patient to buy a certain drug

side effect unwanted reaction to a drug

Find Out More

Books to Read

Bryant-Mole, Karen. *Talking About Drugs*. New York: Raintree
    Steck Vaughn, 2000.

Stanley, Debbie. *Marijuana and Your Lungs: The Incredibly Disgusting Story*.
    New York: Rosen, 2000.

Web Sites

- D.A.R.E. (Drug Abuse Resistance Education) has a Web site for students at www.dare.com/kids/index_3.htm.

- Kidshealth.org (www.kidshealth.org/kid) is a Web site sponsored by the Nemours Foundation and devoted to various topics for students.

- The National Institute on Drug Abuse Web site is at www.drugabuse.gov/NIDAhome.html.

- The Partnership for a Drug-Free America Web site is at www.drugfree.org.

Facts About Drugs

- For a long time, people did not know how **addictive** some drugs were. Until 1929, Coca-Cola contained a small amount of coca—the ingredient used to make **cocaine**.
- Drugs can be very dangerous if they are mixed. When alcohol is taken with some medicines for colds or allergies, it can cause extreme sleepiness. When taken with the pain reliever acetaminophen (or Tylenol), it can increase the person's risk of liver damage.

Index